CENGAGE Learning

Short Stories for Students, Volume 9

Staff

Editorial: Ira Mark Milne, *Editor*. Tim Akers, Angela Y. Jones, Michael LaBlanc, Polly Vedder, *Contributing Editors*. Dwayne D. Hayes, *Managing Editor*.

Research: Victoria B. Cariappa, *Research Team Manager*. Cheryl Warnock, *Research Specialist*. Corrine A. Boland, Tamara Nott, Tracie A. Richardson, *Research Associates*. Timothy Lehnerer, Patricia Love, *Research Assistants*.

Permissions: Maria Franklin, *Permissions Manager*. Margaret A. Chamberlain, Kimberly Smilay, *Permissions Specialist*. Kelly Quin, *Permissions Associate*. Sandra K. Gore, Erin Bealmear, *Permissions Assistants*.

Production: Mary Beth Trimper, *Production Director*. Evi Seoud, *Assistant Production Manager*. Stacy Melson, *Production Assistant*.

Imaging and Multimedia Content Team: Randy Bassett, *Image Database Supervisor*. Robert Duncan, Michael Logusz, *Imaging Specialists*. Pamela A. Reed, *Imaging Coordinator*.

Product Design Team: Cynthia Baldwin, *Product Design Manager*. Pamela A. E. Galbreath, *Senior Art Director*. Gary Leach, *Graphic Artist*.

coordination, expression, arrangement, and classification of information. All rights to this publication will be vigorously defended.

Copyright 2000
The Gale Group
27500 Drake Road
Farmington Hills, Ml 48331-3535

This book is printed on acid-free paper that meets the minimum requirements of American National Standard for Information Sciences—Permanence Paper for Printed Library Materials, ANSI Z39.48-1984.

ISBN 0-7876-3609-6
ISSN 1092-7735

Printed in the United States of America
10 9 8 7 6 5

Two Kinds

Amy Tan

1989

Introduction

"Two Kinds" is the last story in the second of four sections of Amy Tan's immensely successful first book, *The Joy Luck Club*. Tan intended the book to be read as a loose collection of interrelated stories, but it is often referred to as a novel. Several of the stories appeared in periodicals separately, many of them in *Atlantic Monthly,* which purchased the serial rights to the book prior to its publication. "Two Kinds" was initially published in the *Atlantic* in February 1989, one month before the book was released.

Like all the stories in the book, "Two Kinds" is concerned with the complex relationships between mothers and daughters. In particular, Tan's subject is the distance between mothers who were born in China before the communist revolution and thus have been cut off from their native culture for decades, and their American born daughters who must negotiate the twin burdens of their Chinese ancestry and American expectations for success.

In this story, the narrator, Jing-mei, resists her overbearing mother's desire to make her into a musical prodigy in order to compete with one of her friend's daughters. The narrator recalls these events after a period of more than twenty years and still struggles to understand her mother's motivations.

"Two Kinds" contains all the elements that won Tan the well-deserved praise she received for her first book. It shows off her keen ear for the fractured English of the older generation (Tan was trained as a linguist, after all), and her sharp eye for detail in recreating the domestic scenery of mothers and daughters, especially in her descriptions of food and clothing.

Author Biography

Amy Tan was born in 1952 in Oakland, California, to Daisy and John Tan. Her Chinese name, An-mei, means "Blessing from America," and she is the only daughter in the Tan family. Her parents' experiences as immigrants became the basis of her fiction.

When her father and her older brother died of brain tumors within eight months of each other, Tan's world changed. Her mother returned to her old Chinese beliefs and religious practices and became convinced that the family's house in Santa Clara was cursed. Consequently, she packed up her remaining son and daughter and took them on a rambling tour of the East Coast and Europe. Eventually they settled in Montreux, where Amy attended and graduated from high school.

A rebellious teenager, Tan chafed at her mother's insistence that she attend a conservative Baptist college in Oregon and she quickly transferred to San Jose City College and then to San Jose State. She further disappointed her mother by changing her major from pre-med to English and linguistics.

By this time, she was married to a tax lawyer and drifting toward a doctoral degree when she decided to pursue other interests. After a couple of false starts she found considerable success as a freelance business writer.

After a period of introspection and a new interest in her mother's life and stories from China, Tan began writing fiction. She found support in a San Francisco writer's group and found an agent after publishing only one story. Her first book, *The Joy Luck Club*, of which "Two Kinds" is a part, was an astonishing success, and is often credited with sparking the public's interest in Asian American literature. Since then she has written two more novels, two, children's books, and several essays. She lives and works in San Francisco, where she still meets regularly with her writing group.

Plot Summary

In the story "Two Kinds," the narrator is a Chinese American girl who is locked in a struggle over her identity with her Chinese immigrant mother, who believes "that you could be anything you wanted to be in America." This particular struggle invokes the mother's attempt to mold her daughter, Jing-mei, into a musical prodigy so that she will be able to brag to her friend Lindo Jong, whose daughter is a precocious chess champion.

The idea for piano lessons comes from television and popular magazines. The narrator and her mother watch Shirley Temple movies and try to imagine her as a child star. They even go so far as to get her hair styled to make her look like the blond, curly-haired Temple. The mother also reads countless "stories about remarkable children" in the magazines she brings home from people whose houses she cleans.

The mother's vague ambitions for her daughter take shape one night when they are both watching the Ed Sullivan Show (a long-running and popular variety show in the 1960s). There they see "a little Chinese girl, about nine years old, with a Peter Pan haircut," playing a piano solo in a fluffy white dress.

Sure enough, just three days after the watching the show, the narrator's mother has already arranged to trade housecleaning for piano lessons with Mr. Chong, the retired piano teacher in the building. A fierce struggle ensues between the mother's desire to make her daughter into a prodigy (more to satisfy her own ego), and the daughter's resistance to her mother's efforts to make her into someone she is not.

The narrator's strategy is one of quiet and passive resistance. She lies about her practice time and does only what she has to do during her lessons. Subsequently, her mother has no idea how poor and undisciplined a musician she is. At her piano recital, her awful, unpracticed playing embarrasses herself as well as her mother.

Much to the Jing-mei's shock, however, her mother insists that the piano lessons continue. With her mother literally dragging her to the bench to practice, the narrator says that she wishes she weren't her mother's daughter, that she wishes she had been one of the babies her mother abandoned long ago in China.

Such a cruel and hurtful statement silences her mother and ends the piano lessons for good. Many years later, the mother offers to give the piano to her daughter, now in her thirties, who interprets it as a kind of peace offering, though she still does not fully understand her mother's motivations.

Mr. Chong

Mr. Chong—also known as Old Chong—is Jing-mei's deaf and partially blind piano teacher. When she realizes that he can't hear the music, she stops trying to hit the right notes; when she sees that he can't read fast enough to follow the sheet music, she just keeps up the rhythm and he is pleased. At her disastrous recital he is the only one who cheers enthusiastically.

Father

The narrator's father makes only a token appearance in the story. He is not involved in the mother-daughter struggle over piano lessons. He does attend the recital; in fact, the narrator can't tell if he is horrified or silently amused at her performance.

Jing-mei

Jing-mei is a rebellious child caught between two cultures: the Chinese culture that prevails in her mother's home; and the American one that prevails everywhere else. She resists her mother's attempts at discipline and resents the pressures of high achievement that immigrant parents typically place on their children.

She also understands that her mother is using her to win a competition with her friend Lindo Jong; both women brag about whose daughter is more talented. She is resolved to be true to herself and not take part in such a competition. Refusing to practice the piano, she tells her mother that she wishes she were dead, like the babies she knows her mother was forced to abandon when she fled China. She regrets saying such hurtful things later.

Lindo Jong

Also called Auntie Lindo, she is married to Uncle Tin and is the mother of Waverly, the precocious chess prodigy who is the narrator's rival. Lindo goads the narrator's mother into bragging about her daughter's dubious musical talent.

Waverly Jong

"Chinatown's Littlest Chinese Chess Champion," Waverly Jong is Auntie Lindo's daughter. She and the narrator have grown-up together and have long been competing with one another.

Mother

The narrator's mother is a Chinese immigrant who wants her daughter to have the best of both worlds: Chinese tradition and American opportunity. Like many mothers, however, she has a tendency to try to make her daughter into her own image rather than allow her to develop into her own person.

The mother's hopes for her daughter's future belies her own tragic past, however. Like Tan's own mother, the mother in "Two Kinds" was forced to leave her three children behind when she fled an abusive marriage in her native China. By the end of the story, Jing-mei better understands her mother's sacrifices and motivations.

Old Chong

See Mr. Chong

Media Adaptations

- "Two Kinds" is a part of the film version of *The Joy Luck Club*. Tan wrote the screenplay (with Ronald

Bass) for this adaptation of her novel. The film was released in 1993 and directed by Wayne Wang. It was released on videocassette in 1994 and is available from Buena Vista Home Video.

- "Two Kinds" also appears in the (abridged) audiocassette version of the book, available from Dove Books Audio and narrated by the author.

Themes

American Dream

Anthropologists and other scholars who study the immigrant experience in America have long noted that the American dream exerts a powerful influence on new arrivals in the country. These scholars have also pointed out the burden of these dreams usually falls more heavily upon the shoulders of American-born children of immigrants.

Often immigrant parents are willing to sacrifice everything, including careers, family, and property, to pursue new lives in America. Realizing that they may not achieve the American dream of material success and social acceptance, they tend to transfer those ambitions to their children.

The narrator's mother in "Two Kinds," for example, insists that "you could be anything you wanted to be in America." She ticks off the possibilities to her daughter: "You could open a restaurant. You could work for the government and get good retirement. You could buy a house with almost no money down. You could become rich. You could become instantly famous."

While such pressures on the second-generation of immigrant families is common to all ethnic groups in America, the mother in "Two Kinds" and other Chinese American women of her generation were particularly interested in their daughters' success. The women of Jing-mei's (and Tan's) mother's generation grew up in rigidly patriarchal China and were expected to be subservient and silent even in America. Though they feared the effects of liberal American culture on their daughters, they also wished to live vicariously through them and pressured them to succeed in ways they could not have imagined.

As critic E. D. Huntley puts it, these "mothers have borne daughters, and invested in them all of the hopes and dreams that have propelled the older generation across an ocean to America. To give those daughters the best that the New World can offer the mothers have sacrificed their youth and their homeland."

The problem arises, however, when the daughters want to make choices of their own. As Huntley maintains, "the daughters see in their mothers not nurturing angels, only stern disciplinarians, domineering and possessive women who refuse to relinquish any maternal control."

Identity

When Jing-mei's mother says to her daughter in the opening paragraph of "Two Kinds," "you could be anything you wanted to be in America," she really means that her daughter could be anything her mother decided she could be. There are many aspects to the cultural and generational gap that separates Jing-mei from her mother (and the other mothers and daughter in *The Joy Luck Club),* but the one featured in the story entitled "Two Kinds" is the question of identity.

For Jing-mei's mother identity is not problematic; even in California she identifies herself as a Chinese wife and mother. She also strives to maintain Chinese traditions and beliefs in her new culture. Her intersections with American cultural are transitory and superficial and do not require her to reconsider or reconfigure her identity.

Since most of her contact with American culture is through the popular media like magazines and television, she can be a passive and uncritical receptor of new ideas. It's not so simple for her daughter, however, who has to move across cultural boundaries and obstacles that her mother cannot begin to appreciate.

Writing about generational differences in *The Joy Luck Club* as a whole, Walter Shear observes that in each story "the focus is either on a mother, who figures out her world, or on the daughters, who seem caught in a sophisticated cultural trap, knowing possibilities rather than answers, puzzling over the realities that seem to be surrounding them and trying to find their place in an ambivalent world."

The mother-daughter struggle over identity in "Two Kinds" is less about who Jing-mei will turn out to be, prodigy or not, and more about their different beliefs about the nature and mechanisms of identity. Jing-mei's mother, for whom destiny and biology were synonymous with identity, believes fiercely but naively that she can invent her daughter's identity.

For Jing-mei, identity is not something put on or invented, it's something essential and individual. The mother and daughter have completely opposite understandings of identity and individuality, making their conflicts inevitable. As the narrator says later in the story, "Unlike my mother, I did not believe I could be anything I wanted to be. I could only be me."

Style

Memoir

All the stories in *The Joy Luck Club* are interlocking personal narratives in different voices. Because the narrators appear as characters in each other's stories, as well as tell their own stories, Tan does not have to fully develop the narrator's voice in each story. Nevertheless, the stories can stand alone, and "Two Kinds" was published separately; therefore it is possible to discuss the narrative technique utilized in the story.

In "Two Kinds" the perspective moves back and forth between the adult and the child. In this way, Tan tells the story through the child's innocent view and the adult's experienced eyes. This allows readers to make judgments of their own, to add their own interpretations of the mother-daughter struggle.

This literary device also invites readers to think about the way memory itself functions, how we use events in the past to help make sense of our present. Literary critic Ben Xu explains that "it is not just that we have 'images,' 'pictures,' and 'views' of ourselves in memory, but that we also have 'stories' and narratives to tell about the past which both shape and convey our sense of self. Our sense of what has happened to us is entailed not in actual happening but in meaningful happenings, and the meanings of our past experience ... are constructs produced in much the same way that narrative is produced."

Topics for Further Study

- What does Jing-mei expect will happen at the recital? Does she plan to give the kind of performance that she gives? Why or why not?

- Why is the narrator's mother so fixated on making her daughter into some kind of prodigy? Besides the competition with Lindo Jong, what larger cultural forces may be encouraging her to think this way?

- At the end of the story the narrator notices that the piece of music that she struggled with as a child ("Pleading Child") has a companion piece, "Contented Child." She realizes that they are "two halves of the same song." Explain how this can be understood as a metaphor for the story.

- A recurring theme in Tan's work is the difficulty of assimilation into American society for many immigrants. Research your own family history and, if possible, gather stories from your family history. What problems did your family encounter as they assimilated into American culture? What traditions have survived the assimilation process?

In other words memory is a two-way street; it shapes the story as much as the story makes the memory. In Xu's words, "memory is not just a narrative, even though it does have to take a narrative form; it is more importantly an experiential relation between the past and the present, projecting a future as well."

Talk Story

While American daughters like Jing-mei employ personal narrative as a way of telling stories, the Chinese mothers in Tan's stories find it more difficult to talk about themselves. The specific and innovative strategy that Tan uses to voice the mother's experiences is borrowed from Chinese folk tradition, the talk story.

E. D. Huntley defines talk story as "a narrative strategy for those characters whose ties to Chinese tradition remain strong." It allows these characters to "draw on traditional oral forms to shape their stories and to disguise the urgency and seriousness with which they are attempting to transmit to their daughters the remnants of a culture that is fading even from their own lives."

This means that the mothers, "who have been socialized into silence for most of their lives," learn to "reconfigure the events of these lives into acceptable public utterances: painful experiences are recast in the language of folk tale; cautionary reminders become gnomic phrases; real life takes on the contours of myth." Because this indirect means is the only way Jing-mei's mother can interpret and express her experiences, she is shocked into silence when her daughter speaks directly about the daughters she abandoned in China years earlier.

Historical Context

Chinese Immigration to America

San Francisco was (and still is) one of the largest Chinese American communities in the United States. When immigrant groups settle in one area and create extensive social and economic structures, these areas are called enclaves. By the time the mothers in *The Joy Luck Club* (and Tan's own parents) arrived in California, there was a large and thriving Chinese American enclave.

The first wave of Chinese immigrants to the United States occurred in the latter half of the nineteenth century. Until the passage of the Chinese Exclusion Act of 1882, which was designed to limit the numbers of Chinese entering the country and prevented those already here from becoming citizens, as many as 30,000 a year arrived in the United States from mainland China.

These immigrants were almost exclusively male and "only the hardest, dirtiest, most menial jobs were open to them," according to social historian Thomas Sowell. They built most of the railroad across the Sierra and took on the dangerous jobs of strikebreakers in the mines. Nonetheless, they maintained strong social ties and were able to establish economic structures such as mutual aid societies and credit unions.

When the Chinese Exclusion act was finally repealed in 1943, more women arrived from China and the sex imbalance (and seedy reputation) of Chinatowns improved. The population of Chinese Americans began to rise and by 1950 it was higher than its earlier peak in 1890. These children, like Jing-mei in "Two Kinds" were often expected to make significant strides up the American social and economic ladder.

Although they escaped the anti-Chinese laws and overt prejudice that faced earlier generations, they still encountered a whole range of difficulties associated with biculturalism: "cultural dislocation; the problems and challenges of integrating two cultures; intergenerational struggles within immigrant families; the conflict between acculturation and adherence to an ancestral tradition, and between assimilation and parochialism," in Huntley's words.

Asian American Literature

The conflicts and tensions associated with biculturalism are a recurring theme of Asian American literature. Tan's unique contribution to the literature is the articulation of the Chinese American woman's voice. Critics and social historians have noted that Chinese women are acculturated to silence and are unlikely to speak or write publicly about private experience.

Chinese American women writers, in Huntley's estimation, "have been largely but inadvertently responsible for the new and sudden popularity of Asian American writing, a development made even more startling because Chinese woman were an almost invisible minority in American society until the early 1950s."

Following the lead of Maxine Hong Kingston, Tan developed literary and narrative techniques like the use of the talk story that allowed the individual experiences of the older generation of women to be expressed in mythic and symbolic terms. Tan's other major contribution to the genre is the use of many narrators in a single text, a device that Hong Kingston had already introduced American readers to in *The Woman Warrior: Memoirs of a Girlhood Among Ghosts*.

Despite her identification with other Asian American writers and the subject matter of her work, Tan is reluctant to be seen as a writer of ethnic American literature. In an interview in on-line magazine *Salon,* Tan explained her position. "Placing on writers the responsibility to represent a culture is an onerous burden. Someone who writes fiction is not necessarily writing a depiction of any generalized group, they're writing a very specific story." Nevertheless, the commercial and critical success of Tan's work is often credited with sparking a new interest among publishers and readers in Asian American writing.

Critical Overview

Early reviews of Tan's *The Joy Luck Club*, often mistakenly called a novel, were generally positive. Writing for the *New York Times Book Review*, Orville Schell praises Tan's grasp of the Chinese American experience and says that Tan "has a wonderful eye for what is telling, a fine ear for dialog, a deep empathy for her subject matter and a guilelessly straightforward way of writing." The stories, he claims, "sing with a rare fidelity and beauty."

In a review in *Time* magazine, John Skow maintains that "the author writes with both inside and outside knowing, and her novel rings clearly, like a fine porcelain bowl."

Some reviewers were less impressed with Tan's narrative structure, however. Writing in *New York* magazine, Rhoda Koenig finds the book "lively and bright but not terribly deep," and notes that "some of the stories resolve themselves too neatly and cozily." She concedes, however, that "one cannot help being charmed ... by the sharpness of the observation."

Similarly, Carole Angier in *New Statesman and Society* asserts that the book is "over-schematic," that "in the end it gives you indigestion, as if you've eaten too any Chinese fortune cookies, or read too many American Mother's Day cards."

In the decade since its publication, Tan's collection of stories has remained a critical and commercial success. Its popular success has helped open the doors of the publishing industry to other Asian American authors. Though it remains too soon to tell how literary history will assess the stories in *The Joy Luck Club,* the book has already received a great deal of attention in critical journals and has been the subject of numerous master's theses and doctoral dissertations in recent years.

E. D. Huntley contends that the "proliferation of scholarly examinations ... points to the literary and cultural value of Tan's work." She goes on to assert that "Tan has already earned herself a berth in the canon of contemporary American literature," and that "Tan's novels have proven both their literary staying power as well as their broad appeal to a wide readership."

What Do I Read Next?

- *The Woman Warrior* (1976) is Maxine Hong Kingston's memoir of her bicultural childhood. Tan cites it as an influence on her fiction.

- Another story that inspired Tan is Louise Erdrich's *Love Medicine* (1984). The novel chronicles the story of two Native American families.

- Gus Lee's *China Boy* (1991) is a semi-autobiographical novel.

Sources

Angier, Carole. Review, in *New Statesman and Society,* June 30, 1989, p. 35.

Huntley, E. D. *Amy Tan: A Critical Companion,* Westport, CT: Greenwood Press, 1998.

Koenig, Rhoda. Review, in *New York,* March 20, 1989, p. 82.

Kristeva, Julia. "The Meaning of Grief," in *Black Sun: Depression and Melancholia,* New York: Columbia University Press, 1989.

Schell, Orville. "Your Mother is in Your Bones," in *The New York Times Book Review,* March 19, 1989, pp. 3, 28.

Shear, Walter. "Generational Differences and the Diaspora in *The Joy Luck Club,* " in *Critique,* Vol. 34, No. 3, Spring 1993, pp. 193-99.

Skow, John. "Tiger Ladies in *The Joy Luck Club,* " in *Time,* March 27, 1989, p. 98.

Sowell, Thomas. *Ethnic America: A History,* New York: Basic Books, Inc., 1981, pp. 133-54.

Xu, Ben. "Memory and the Ethnic Self: Reading Amy Tan's *The Joy Luck Club,* " in *MELUS,* Vol. 19, No. 1, pp. 3-16.

Further Reading

Kim, Elaine. *Asian American Literature: An Introduction to the Writings and Their Social Context,* Philadelphia: Temple University Press, 1982.

> An influential and ground-breaking study, this remains an essential work in the field and provides an excellent introduction to major authors and critical issues.

CPSIA information can be obtained
at www.ICGtesting.com
Printed in the USA
BVHW042021300720
585040BV00006B/596

9 781375 395380